GOETHE

TWO ADDRESSES
BY
ALBERT SCHWEITZER

Goethe

TWO ADDRESSES
BY
ALBERT SCHWEITZER

Translated by
CHARLES R. JOY and C. T. CAMPION
with an introduction by
CHARLES R. JOY
Editor, *Albert Schweitzer: An Anthology*

1948

THE BEACON PRESS · BOSTON

TO

EMMY MARTIN

The grace of the Munster Valley
is yours as well
The fires of mercy which you feed
burn within you

PREFATORY NOTE

The two addresses on Johann Wolfgang von Goethe here published were delivered by Albert Schweitzer on important occasions. Both of them were spoken in Goethe's natal city, Frankfort on the Main. The first of them, chronologically, was given on August 28, 1928, when Frankfort bestowed the Goethe Prize on Dr. Schweitzer in the Goethe House. The second was given on March 22, 1932, at the University of Frankfort, on the one hundredth anniversary of Goethe's death. The first address was translated into English by Mr. C. T. Campion, published in the *Hibbert Journal*, and afterwards circulated in America in a paper-bound leaflet. The second, issued by the C. H. Beck Publishing House in Munich, is here for the first time translated into English.

The order in which these two addresses appear in this book is the reverse of their chronological order. It seems fitting that the longer, more general, and more adequate study of Goethe's life, character, and literary genius should precede the shorter address in which Schweitzer acknowledges his own indebtedness to Goethe.

These addresses are important, not so much as a contribution to our understanding of Goethe, as they are for their contribution to our understanding of Schweitzer. The surprising similarity in the life and foundation principles of these two great men, living a century apart, is set forth clearly in the two addresses, and still further emphasized in the introduction.

It is the belief of the editor and translators that Schweitzer's life and activities can be comprehended only in the light of these two lectures.

—CHARLES R. JOY

Newton Highlands,
Massachusetts
1948

ACKNOWLEDGMENT

Grateful acknowledgment is made to Henry Holt and Company, Inc., N.Y., for permission to reprint copyrighted material from *Out of My Life and Thought* by Albert Schweitzer.

CONTENTS

INTRODUCTION

GOETHE AND SCHWEITZER: TWO OLYMPIANS

"No one can write his real religious life with pen or pencil. It is written only in actions, and its seal is our own character, not our orthodoxy." This is Dr. Wilfred Thomason Grenfell speaking. He and Albert Schweitzer are kindred souls. One devoted his life to the fishermen of the frozen north, and the other to the natives of the equatorial jungle, but the same glowing motivation lies at the core of their hearts. "Whether we, our neighbor, or God is the judge," Grenfell continues, "absolutely the only value of our 'religious' life to ourselves or to anyone is what it fits us for and enables us to do. Creeds, when expressed only in words, clothes, or abnormal lives, are daily growing less acceptable as passports to Paradise. What my particular intellect can accept cannot commend me to God. His 'well done' is only spoken to the man who 'wills to do His will.' "

The world has an insatiable curiosity (or is it an abiding concern?), to know the reasons which lead men to forsake comfort and affluence and prestige to found hospitals at St. Anthony in Labrador or at Lambaréné on the banks of the Ogowé River. It is not easy for the ordinary man to understand. The children of St. Francis have always been considered a bit mad by their contemporaries. It is much easier to comprehend the rich young man of the parable who went away sorrowing because he could not give up his privileged position to take the hard road of discipleship.

Albert Schweitzer has explained the reasons why he left his important teaching post, his writings in theology and philosophy, the great libraries and old organs of Europe, to study medicine and bury himself in the steaming tropics of Africa. He went because he had no right to happiness while other men suffered, he went to repay a debt which the white races owed to the black, he went because he felt he must make some return for the privileges of his lot, he went because he had to give satisfying expression to the supreme ethics of his life: love in selfless service.

There is something pure and lifted-up about all this, like the holy grail in the Arthurian legends, and if we do not wholly understand, still we do not strive with stained and sullied hands to lift the crimson samite from the golden chalice. There are quiet reserves in the lives of all great men which must be respected. Only when they themselves bid us penetrate into the inner sanctuaries of the soul may we enter.

In these two lectures on Goethe, Albert Schweitzer reveals more frankly than in any other place some of the influences which molded his character. He whom we are beginning to reverence as one of the rare spiritual leaders of all time, humbly acknowledges a debt which is hardly hinted at elsewhere in his writings. He whom we call a master calls himself a disciple, a disciple to the great immortal of German literature, Johann Wolfgang von Goethe. As one of the endearing traits of Schweitzer's character is his profound and sterling humility, it is indeed possible that he overrates the influence of Goethe upon his life. Certainly he does not recognize, or at least he does not underline, the many flaws in Goethe's nature. We who can see both men with some perspective, though one is long dead and the other throbbingly alive, quickly perceive that in moral and spiritual sublimity it is Schweitzer who is the cloisterer and Goethe who is the novice. As one stands on the Quai

Wilson in Geneva and looks across the lake in the late afternoon to the slopes of Le Grand Salève and Le Petit Salève, one may see, if he is fortunate, a rosy glow on eternal snow rising beyond and above. Perhaps, however, we are dealing here with two men, each of whom in his own way is an Olympian, dwelling far above the mist-enshrouded lower hills of Thessaly.

In the light of Schweitzer's own grateful testimony one may not doubt the worth of the heritage which Goethe handed down. One may go further than Schweitzer and point out, as the following pages will attempt to point out, the many striking similarities between the lives of these two men. One may even venture to suggest that Goethe's contribution to Schweitzer's life and thought was greater than Schweitzer himself is aware of. But after one has so daringly ventured, he must inevitably revert to the simple conviction that Schweitzer is a man in his own right, and that on the edge of the primeval forest he has blazed trails through the ethical wilderness of modern life, which may some day be the traveled highways of a better humanity. He is no colorless follower. He himself is a pioneer.

While it is not, therefore, quite true to say that in these two lectures on Goethe Schweitzer is writing his own autobiography, it is nonetheless true that in these lectures one of the missing keys to the understanding of his life is presented. It is when we bring Goethe and Schweitzer face to face that comprehension begins.

With touching humility Schweitzer acknowledges his debt to Goethe. First of all, he recognizes in Goethe a man who has remained loyal to a simple nature-philosophy in a day when the world and nature were being forced by the philosophers into conformity with man's ideas for the sake of harmony. This simple nature-philosophy was Schweitzer's also, and while he does not say that he derived his philosophy from Goethe, he does pay tribute to the man

who, before him, stood guard at a post which most thinkers
had deserted. Both men were humble in the presence of the
phenomena of nature. We must not try to get behind them,
Goethe constantly insisted. "Man's noblest experience is
that of awe, and if the phenomena as such are awe-inspiring,
let him be content. He will mount no higher; he should
not try to get behind the experience." This, too, was
Schweitzer's position. He thought, perhaps erroneously,
that he was the first Westerner who dared to be absolutely
skeptical with regard to our knowledge of the objective
world, without at the same time renouncing the affirmative
ethical attitude. He believed profoundly that any world-
view which was not based on despair of intellectual knowledge must be artificial and fictitious, since it rested on an un-
trustworthy interpretation of the universe.

Goethe, however, was a strange mixture of pagan and
Christian. With his artist friends he copied the paintings
in the wonderful Sistine Chapel in Rome, which was the
coolest place to work in the oppressive heat of August, and
actually dozed in the papal chair. He saw the Pope celebrate
mass at Christmas and Corpus Christi, and then wrote: "I
have grown too old a Diogenes to be in any way impressed.
. . . It is stupid to bolster up a delusion with all this fuss
and feathers, and when I look at all these mummeries as an
artist and as a poet I find them wearisome and trivial, however much they may impress the infantile and sensuous
mind."

Schweitzer could never have uttered these words, nor
could he have dozed on the papal throne. He had too much
respect for the faith and convictions of other men. But he,
too, in his inmost thought was impatient with the empty and
traditional forms of religion. One may search his writings
in vain for any of the old forms of Christian dogma. His
simple faith in the profound principle of Christian love
which he finds in Jesus is unmarred by the theological spec-

ulations of the later centuries. He is sure that the truth that was in the ethics of Jesus can stand alone. It needs no scaffolding round it, no shoring to stay it. Sectarianism means as little to him as it did to Goethe. Christianity is for him chaotic in its very greatness. It is no longer a force in the world. It could not prevent the war. It is shot through with weakness and mistakes. It needs to be filled again to overflowing with the spirit of Jesus if it is to achieve its destined purpose. Yet Schweitzer believes earnestly that the human soul is capable of asserting itself triumphantly over a universe which is both creative and destructive, good and evil, a universe which offers no evidence that man is its goal or even its major concern.

Schweitzer found inspiration in Goethe's *Harzreise* (journey into the Harz Mountains), when in the winter of 1777 Goethe set out through the worst kind of weather to visit a man who needed his help. Again and again in later years, Schweitzer, called upon to undertake some difficult and unpleasant duty, said to himself, "This is a *Harzreise* for you."

At this point, however, Schweitzer idealizes Goethe. The latter's service to humanity was enormous, in actual accomplishment perhaps more significant than Schweitzer's own contribution, but many times Goethe failed in his relations with individuals, refusing to make the *Harzreise* himself, seeking escape from unpleasant duties, and deliberately shunning those kindly human relations in which Schweitzer has found his highest satisfaction and usefulness.

There can be no doubt that Schweitzer found great and constant comfort, when the pressure of hospital duties made his music and his writing and even his thinking impossible, in the fact that Goethe also made the same sacrifice, if sacrifice it be. Goethe came to regard it as his destiny to exhaust himself in the daily round of administrative duties, as before he had found expression for his inmost spirit in the exalted moods of literature. Indeed, he came to think of his poetic gifts as a lovely but quite unrelated matter, and to rejoice in the happy fate that had brought him to his government post at Weimar. With complete devotion and with unremitting zest he entered into the performance of an astonishing variety of duties. He reconstructed the mines at Ilmenau, directed the court theater, he had charge of schools and roads, he built factories and laboratories, tore down a hospital and renovated a castle and strove to introduce economy into the finances of the district. The multitudinous details of his life as they appear in his daily journals are literally astounding. There was nothing too unimportant for him to turn his hand and his mind to.

Occasionally, it is true, the artist in him rebelled. Once he exclaimed: "We poets should be treated as the Dukes of Saxony treated Luther—forbidden to walk the streets, confined in a strong fortress. Would that someone would treat me that way, then my *Tell* would be completed by Michaelmas." At fifty Goethe was director of the court theater and minister of education, but his *Faust* was still unfinished. Then he roused himself, and by extraordinary effort added about 800 lines to what he had written years before. So the first part was ready for publication when he was fifty-two, but he did not actually publish it until he was fifty-nine. Even then it appeared only as a fragment and not another line was added until he was seventy-six. The book was not finished until he was eighty-two, the year of his death.

Goethe took immense satisfaction in his administrative responsibilities; in the midst of a statement to that effect he wrote: "Yet I feel like a snared bird. I have wings and cannot use them." He praised Marcus Aurelius that he did not permit his writing to absorb all his energies, and then, as if involuntarily, added: "So far as I can I am diverting the water from the fountains and cascades to the mills and the irrigation ditches; but while I am not looking some wicked sprite turns the tap and the water all runs away in a torrent. I think I am riding on my hack horse to the station where I must go, and suddenly the mare beneath me turns into a glorious, uncontrollable, winged steed, and off she flies with me."

So also has it been with Schweitzer. He, too, has found his literary, musical and philosophical work completely submerged under the practical burdens of administering his hospital. Digging postholes for new buildings, fighting the traveler ants on their destructive inroads, planting a garden hewn out of the jungle, writing in longhand his many letters, keeping the records of the pharmacy, ordering supplies a year ahead, operating on the sick and burying the dead, teaching and preaching to the natives, always under tremendous pressure, with inadequate assistance and meager support, Schweitzer has carried on his enterprise as a symbol of the Christian love he came into the forest to impart and to exemplify. Reconciled as he has been to arduous labor, there have been fleeting moments of regret that he could not continue or complete some important intellectual undertaking. His work on *The Philosophy of Civilization* still lies unfinished. The first two volumes, *The Decay and Restoration of Civilization*, and *Civilization and Ethics*, appeared in 1923. Still in 1947 the third volume of this, his crowning intellectual endeavor, remains incomplete. Will he finish it? It would be a desolating disappointment to him if this became impossible, but still he continues the incessant and exhausting work of his hospital. In his vision of ministrations of mercy continuing in the primeval forests after he has gone he finds his consolation, just as Faust found it at the very end of his life in his vision of the green meadows and gardens, the woods and towns which he purposes to wrest from the sea for the benefit of the people.

Schweitzer finds inspiration again in Goethe's devotion to natural science. It is a salutary discipline, he insists, for one who has been dealing with intellectual concepts to face the hard facts of life and the universe. Certainly Goethe neglected the supreme gifts of his genius to study all the sciences that reveal the nature of the world: botany, geology, zoölogy, chemistry, physics, anthropology. As Schweitzer points out, he was regarded by his time as only an amateur in these fields of research, but in reality he was much more than that. At the age of thirty-five Goethe discovered the intermaxillary bone in the human cheek, which up to that time had been found only in animals. The science of his day jeered at his conclusion that we could not discern the difference between the brute and the man, only a century afterwards to acclaim it as a great discovery. It was Goethe who glimpsed the Darwinian theory seventy years before Darwin, and proclaimed that every bone was a part or fragment of the vertebral system. Of course, Goethe was sometimes wrong. The theory of light for which he contended valiantly, and sometimes bitterly, until the day of his death was a mistaken theory. The Olympians are not always right.

In like manner Schweitzer turned in the full maturity of his early success to the science of medicine, and found it through all the ensuing years a rewarding, if rigorous, regime. He proved to be a capable practitioner in the field of tropical medicine, and all that he learned and experienced enhanced the spiritual richness of his life.

In two other ways Schweitzer credits Goethe for strong influence upon his life. Goethe has an abiding concern for justice, and in this Schweitzer is one with him. Indeed, Schweitzer's sense of justice far surpasses Goethe's. Goethe's treatment of Friederike is not the sole instance in Goethe's life of gross injustice. When confronted with stern or unpleasant realities Goethe often took refuge in flight; Schweitzer never.

Second, Goethe was a man of his age, trying to share all

of its activities and all of its aspirations. Schweitzer is perhaps less a man of his age than Goethe, if for no other reason than that he is so far removed from the main currents of it. Yet while Goethe comprehended the life of his time in its outward aspects so fully, Schweitzer has penetrated more deeply into the inner spirit of mankind than Goethe ever did. Here it is Schweitzer that is the master.

In one respect both men stand largely aloof from their age. Neither has much respect for the opinions of the multitude. Each has an instinctive disdain for the mob. Neither is moved by the applause or the condemnation of the crowd. Each believes in the individual. In Goethe's letters and journals there is hardly a reference to the mighty disturbances of his time. When the Rhine Confederation was formed he remarked that a quarrel between servants and taxicab drivers on a bridge excited him more than the partition of the Holy Roman Empire. So the stirring events of these recent decades have found little reflection in the writings of Albert Schweitzer. Neither has been much interested in the external pattern of revolution or reform. Goethe wished to partition the great estates for the benefit of the people, but gave up his dream in the end as impossible of achievement, saying: "Meantime one waters his own garden, even though he can not produce rain for the whole country." Schweitzer devotes some attention to the great problems arising from colonization and trade, but has no far-reaching solutions to offer.

Goethe's lip sometimes curled in contempt for men. He quoted with approval Ariosto's comment upon the mob: "They should have been killed at birth." He gave vent to his disillusionment in these words: "We are sure in our younger days that we can build palaces for mankind, but with experience we find that the most we can do is to clean up their dunghills." Schweitzer seldom feels such despair. Once, indeed, in a moment of weariness, he threw himself into a chair in his consulting-room and groaned out, "What a blockhead I was to come out here to doctor savages like these!" But with apparent approval he quotes the quiet rebuke of his Negro orderly, "Yes, Doctor, here on earth you are a great blockhead, but not in heaven."

Any student of the lives of these two men must be aware of other similarities between them, which Schweitzer does not refer to. Both men have a deep and clear-sighted devotion to truth, to truth at any cost. Neither is blinded by the conventions and traditional beliefs of the age, or even of the ages. Goethe once said that the discovery of the earth's motion around the sun was the most sublime discovery ever made by the human mind, "more important than the whole Bible put together." Even stronger, then, than his love for beauty, for the exaltation of poetry, was his love for truth. It is not in any religious faith, not in any creative art, that the clue to his character is to be found. It is to be found in his devotion to science. He was not a Christian, unless you agree with his own daring conjecture that perhaps he was the only Christian.

Schweitzer, too, is a fearless seeker for truth, for truth unshackled. "If thought is to set out on its journey unhampered," he said, "it must be prepared for anything, even for arrival at intellectual agnosticism. But even if our will-to-action is destined to wrestle endlessly and unavailingly with an agnostic view of the universe and of life, still this painful disenchantment is better for it than persistent refusal to think out its position at all. For this disenchantment does, at any rate, mean that we are clear as to what we are doing." In Schweitzer's studies of Jesus and Paul, and in his emphasis upon the central significance of the eschatological element in their thought, the whole structure of Christian theology is shaken. Schweitzer himself well knew that his conclusions would be considered heretical, even blasphemous. He admitted that his views, although they were

reached after much careful and prayerful research, would
not be acceptable to the piety of his day. He makes this
quite clear in *Out of My Life and Thought*, when he
writes: "Since the essential nature of the spiritual is truth,
every new truth means ultimately something won. Truth
is under all circumstances more valuable than nontruth,
and this must apply to truth in the realm of history as
to other kinds of truth. Even if it comes in a guise which
piety finds strange and at first makes difficulties for her, the
final result can never mean injury; it can only mean greater
depth. Religion has, therefore, no reason for trying to avoid
coming to terms with historical truth." The historical Jesus
which Schweitzer uncovered at the end of his quest, was a
man of his time, and not of our time, and only as his spirit,
which is of no time, but of all time, is reborn in our hearts
can the life and teaching of Jesus be of inspiration to us.
Schweitzer never faltered in his search for truth. "Buy the
truth, and sell it not," advised the writer of Proverbs.
Schweitzer would not sell the truth which he had bought
to win the pottage of praise. It was his precious birthright.

Goethe and Schweitzer alike, Christian in no conven-
tional sense of the term, were sure that in the end the truth,
despised, forsworn, disglorified, condemned as impious and
profane, would win the day and set men everlastingly free.

The sure basis of Schweitzer's ethical and religious
thought is his conception of reverence—reverence for life.
In his search for some stable foundation for the palace of
ethics he was building Schweitzer was long baffled. Then,
one day, on a tedious errand of mercy in the African jungle,
he found it. Let Schweitzer describe the experience himself:
"Slowly we crept upstream, laboriously feeling—it was the
dry season—for the channels between the sandbanks. Lost in
thought I sat on the deck of the barge, struggling to find the
elementary and universal conception of the ethical which
I had not discovered in any philosophy. Sheet after sheet I

covered with disconnected sentences, merely to keep myself concentrated on the problem. Late on the third day, at the very moment when, at sunset, we were making our way through a herd of hippopotamuses, there flashed upon my mind, unforeseen and unsought, the phrase, 'Reverence for Life.' The iron door had yielded: the path in the thicket had become visible. Now I had found my way to the idea in which world- and life-affirmation and ethics are contained side by side! Now I knew that the world-view of ethical world- and life-affirmation, together with its ideals of civilization, is founded in thought."

This was to him an ecstatic experience, a transfiguring mount of vision. This was his peak of Darien, from which he gazed in rapture upon a shining, limitless sea. Is it not strange that Schweitzer was unaware of another presence on that peak, that he did not perceive Goethe standing there beside him? For Goethe, too, had caught a glimpse of this truth. He, too, had had his transfiguration hour.

Schweitzer was very familiar with Goethe's *Wilhelm Meister*. He must have read again and again of Wilhelm's visit to the Pedagogic Province, where he is taking his son Felix. Somehow what Goethe had written and taught must have become so integral a part of Schweitzer's subliminal self that he failed to recognize in the words that came to him on the mount the accents of Goethe's voice. How authentic these accents are let the reader judge.

The Three, who represent the Chief, say to Wilhelm: "One thing there is which no child brings into the world with him; and yet it is on this one thing that all depends for making man in every point a man. If you can discover it yourself, speak it out." Wilhelm thought a little while and then shook his head. After a suitable pause, the Three exclaimed: "Reverence!" Wilhelm seemed to hesitate. "Reverence!" cried the Three a second time. "All want it, perhaps you yourself."

The Three then go on to explain the threefold reverence which they inculcate: reverence for that which is above, reverence for that which is around, reverence for that which is below. The religion which depends on reverence for that which is above is called the Ethnic. The religion which depends upon reverence for that which is around is called the Philosophical. The religion which depends upon reverence for that which is below is called the Christian. This reverence for that which is below is the last step which mankind is fitted and destined to take. Out of these three reverences, conclude the Three, springs the highest reverence of all, reverence for oneself.

To say that Schweitzer's idea of reverence for life came originally from *Wilhelm Meister*, although Schweitzer himself has forgotten the spring from which he drank, is not, however, to depreciate Schweitzer's originality. For Schweitzer has taken that fundamental idea and has developed it into a complete ethical system. There is no indication in *Wilhelm Meister* that Goethe ever carried his idea of reverence to the far point of vision which Schweitzer reaches. With Schweitzer the essential characteristic of reverence is its boundlessness. It includes all that lives, not only that which is above, and that which is around, but the humblest of living creatures, the toad in the posthole, the gnat flying about the lamp, the worm in the road, the flower by the wayside. Goethe thinks of reverence for that which is beneath as reverence for the earth which nourishes us. Schweitzer thinks of it as reverence for the mosquito that stings us, the snake that bites us, the bacterium that kills us. He recognizes the insoluble enigmas which such a view presents, but the reverence he teaches is limitless.

Here, then, are the two Olympians, so much alike in many ways, so profoundly different beneath their likenesses: Goethe brilliant, self-confident, proud, autocratic; Schweitzer simple, humble, lovable, democratic. Goethe the

great master of prose and poetry, and the oft-erring but
deeply discerning student of life; Schweitzer the great master of music and medicine, and the sublime exemplar of
ethical living.

We may ask, again, as many have asked before, why in
one case all the preoccupation with architects and engineers,
with highways and school systems, with forests and
finances, while the one incomparable literary talent within
him was treated as a lovely but irrelevant thing, and in the
other case why all the clearing of the jungle and the planting of gardens, why all the building of hospitals and the
nursing of the sick, while the sweet harmonies of his spirit
and the noble thinking of his mind lay partly dormant and
unexpressed? The answer is as simple and as forthright as it
is profound. Life itself is the greatest thing! Greater far than
its poetry and prose, greater far than its music and its mus-
ings! Life itself can be an epic poem or a soul-stirring sym-
phony! To create a life is to create beauty, to plant a garden
in a wilderness, an oasis in a desert, a shrine in a city slum!
Life is written in deeds, not in words! Its sevenfold seal is its
character!

—CHARLES R. JOY

GOETHE:

**A MEMORIAL ADDRESS
DELIVERED AT THE CELEBRATION
OF THE ONE HUNDREDTH ANNIVERSARY OF HIS DEATH
IN HIS NATIVE CITY, FRANKFORT ON THE MAIN
MARCH 22, 1932**

A HUNDRED YEARS AGO TODAY, at nine o'clock in the morning, Goethe raises himself in his arm-chair, and believing himself to be on the road to recovery, asks what day it is. When he learns that it is the twenty-second of March he says: "Then the spring has begun, and I shall get better all the sooner."

He does not recall then that the twenty-second of March long seemed to him a fateful day; he does not remember that unlucky twenty-second of March in the year 1825, when the Weimar Theater, where Schiller had produced in collaboration with him such splendid performances, went up in flames. Delight in the spring sun shining from the skies fills his whole being.

Then his thoughts begin to wander again, but in a moment of regained consciousness he asks that a shutter which has remained closed should be opened that more light might come in. Before the sun of spring has reached the midday zenith, he has entered into the kingdom of everlasting light.

The city of Frankfort remembers its greatest son on the hundredth anniversary of his death, once more in the brilliant sunshine of spring . . . but also in the greatest emergency that this city and Goethe's people have ever known.

The spiritual life is threatened by the material life. So much that was being done recently for civilization and for culture must now be discontinued. The hundredth anniversary of the death of Goethe occurs at a moment when the public school system, which constituted the pride of his people, and to the furtherance of which for over half a century he contributed unstintingly, a school-system so peculiarly distinguished, begins to disintegrate.

Even the rejoicing which naturally arises among us—because for the first time Frankfort is celebrating a Goethe festival on the property of the university which the sacrificial devotion of its citizens made possible, and upon which, as the city of Goethe, it has a just claim, can hardly find expression. Anxious concern for the future of that university envelops our happiness with gloom. I pray that the good fortune of sister universities which began in the years of deepest necessity and afterwards achieved the most splendid prosperity may be hers also!

May kindly fortune also watch over the ancient and honorable homes of wisdom in Frankfort and keep them safe through all of this trying period!

I hope, moreover, that it may be possible to preserve from ruin the home where Goethe was born, the foundations of which are threatened. The completion of work which is most urgently needed is now rendered uncertain for lack of material.

So pressing are the necessities and the anxieties of this time, that the question might arise whether we should not let this day pass by in silence. The answer is found in *Faust*. There the emperor, still suffering from the effects of the turmoil of battle, gives to the lord high chancellor permission to hold the festival he requests. He says:

"Zwar fühl' ich mich zu ernst, auf Festlichkeit zu sinnen. Doch sei's. . . ." [1]

So let it be.

------

[1] "My mood is still too stern to contemplate a feast.
Still let it be."

It is with peculiarly mixed feelings, however, that we do honor to Goethe today. Proudly we remind ourselves of those imperishable and invaluable elements which we find in him and in his works. At the same time we cannot but ask if he has not become a stranger to us, since the age in which his life and labor fell knew as yet nothing of the needs and problems of our time. Does not the clear light that streams from him shine on to the coming days, which once more will reach the heights where he dwelt, without penetrating into the dark valley where we live?

But away at once with such questions. May that sadness also be banished from this hour which overcomes us when, mindful of the very happy circumstances in which his talents found a peculiarly splendid development, we contemplate those who were unable to bestow upon the world the riches which were theirs because they were snatched away by the war before they were even men, as well as those to whom it is not given to disclose their inner treasure because the destitution in which they live makes it quite impossible.

So great is our grief that we have developed the ability to escape from ourselves, to find inspiration in the knowledge that men once lived their lives under circumstances which permitted them to realize their full manhood, a situation that has become almost incomprehensible to us. Today in such a spirit we approach Goethe, who more than almost any other soul was permitted to live under such favorable circumstances.

*

Goethe himself fully recognizes how much he is indebted to the circumstances in which his life was passed. Many a time, indeed, he speaks about it, the last time only three weeks before his death, in a conversation with the young Genevese Soret to whom we owe such valuable sketches of the last ten years of his life.

He is stimulated as he grows up in rich and manifold ways by what he receives from his native city, so hospitable to the social and spiritual life of the time. Once, indeed, he says himself that he could not imagine another place so favorable in this sense for his cradle. Afterwards in Weimar he finds the special preconditions for the spiritual life, as they can only exist at the courts of princes, preconditions which both the great and the little German courts of that time, as seats of the noblest culture, provided in very extraordinary measure. He lives in an age when men were upheld by the spirit of progress then at work. What a ring those passages in *Dichtung und Wahrheit* have for us today, in which he informs us that he may be taken as proof that in his youth mutual relations were growing ever better, and thoughts of humanity dominated men! And when then he lives through the tremendous upheavals that followed the French Revolution, which seem to endanger the wholesome development of European manhood, he is able to affirm at last, as he witnesses the end of them, that they were something of transient significance.

He does not come to know material cares. He is spared the fight for existence, for which he is not equipped by nature.

He finds in turn both work and leisure in his place at Weimar in just the measure that each of them is necessary for his development. He is able to serve without ever becoming a vassal; he is able to take part in the government as one who is simply concerned for what is just and useful, without being compelled to waste his strength in coming to terms with parties and party opinions.

At the auspicious moments the people whom he needed in his life enter into it. Herder, Wieland, Lessing, Shakespeare, Spinoza and Jacobi give him whatever they have to give.

In Weimar the prince seeks to anticipate his wishes at

every point in friendly understanding so far as it is possible
for him. It is no empty form of words, when Goethe writes
on one occasion: "This prince gave me a chance to develop,
which would not have been possible under conditions exist-
ing anywhere else in my native land."

His friendship with Schiller comes to blossom in 1794
at the very moment when he no longer knows how to escape
from the solitude which he has chosen after his return from
Italy, and when, lacking the creative impulse, he begins to
doubt his poetic talent.

It is indeed true that each of those, whether great or
small, who help him on his way, receives in the end more
from him than he gives to them. But he himself, prisoner to
those manifold uncertainties and indecisions which are so
conspicuously associated with the strength of his will and
his creative art, needed those who would bring to him kindness, understanding, encouragement, and companionship.
That he always found these things from the years of youth
to the loneliness of age is the great good fortune that rules
his life. Hardly one of the great books that contribute to
the perfection of his work would have been possible without inspiration and support in the joy of the task from
someone who understood. It was his sister in *Götz von Berlichingen*, his father in *Egmont*, and Schiller in *Faust* and
so many other books.

*

Far be it from us confronted by such human personality
to let ourselves go in undiscriminating wonder. There is a
great deal in Goethe's life, in his thought, in his work, that
we should like to eliminate, very much also that we should
like to add to.

Goethe is not an ideal form which directly attracts and
inspires. He is less than that and he is more than that.

The fundamental characteristics of his personality are

always honesty and sincerity. He may well profess, and he has done so, that lying, hypocrisy and intrigue are as alien to him as vanity, envy and ingratitude.

Around both of these qualities, which determined the course of his life, move other qualities which are not reconciled with one another, but rather spring from the two opposite poles of spontaneity and non-spontaneity. In one moment Goethe is charmingly communicative, and then immediately afterwards he becomes taciturn. He is by nature very kind but he can in turn be very cool. He takes the most extreme and lively delight in everything he experiences, and immediately afterwards is frankly and anxiously concerned lest he lose his equilibrium. He is impulsive and at the same time indecisive. In his letter of August 27, 1794, to Schiller, he informs his new friend, that upon a closer acquaintanceship he will discover a certain moodiness and hesitancy in him which he has never been able to master.

Richly endowed with talent, as Goethe also is, he is not by birth either a happy or a harmonious nature, and he has to labor with himself, a labor which is not made easier by the fact that he has many periods of sickness, through which he lost, according to his own testimony, "some of the best years of his life." And how long he was held up by the despondency and inability to work which follow in the train of such illnesses!

Goethe sees that the way he must take is this, not to impose upon himself anything foreign to his nature, but to let whatever good in him lives and smoulders develop, and to lay aside whatever is not good in him.

He devotes himself with deepest intensity to this self-discipline. In *Dichtung und Wahrheit* he speaks of the inner earnestness with which even in his earlier years he regarded the world and himself. Everyone who comes into touch with him and understands him is impressed by this earnestness.

Disciplining himself in this way Goethe attains a manhood which is based on truth and sincerity and is distinguished by the absence of envy, by composure, peaceableness, and kindliness.

Life offers him rich opportunities to give expression to this lack of envy, this composure and peaceableness. It is simply not true that life is a prosperous and easy existence for him. After the appearance of *Werther* none of his productions receives general approbation. The intimate artistry which is manifest in his later poems alienates people. They had expected something very different from the writer of *Götz von Berlichingen* and *Werther*. How many stupid things Goethe had to hear about such a perfect work as *Hermann und Dorothea*, not only from the uncritical masses, but also from those who were intimate with him!

The edition of his collected works which he prepared in Italy has only a very moderate success. His pieces for the stage are hardly played at all. His fame as a poet pales before the ascendancy of Schiller's star. Nobody takes any notice of his researches in the domain of science, for he is not an expert there. Open and covert hostility is active against him.

Quietly and composedly, however, he continues on his way. In a letter to Schelling he ventures to ask the question whether anyone has ever heard him cry out in the midst of all the enmity of which he was the object!

His peaceableness is matched by his kindness. Occasionally, it is true, he is stiff to those who are not so near to him, a stiffness which is taken as coolness and interpreted as pride. This increases with the years as his father's nature comes out ever more clearly in him. At bottom this stiffness, as Chancellor von Müller remarks to Grillparzer, who has been much disappointed in his first visit to Goethe (September 29, 1826), is only his own embarrassment, caused by his frequent association with little known or unknown people. On his second visit to Goethe two days later Grill-parzer, in fact, is able to affirm "that Goethe is now just as warm and lovable as recently he was stiff and cold."

True to his deepest nature Goethe is throughout his whole life affectionate and sympathetic. He never withholds himself from anyone who really needs him. This we have from many witnesses. He tries to be especially helpful in every case of spiritual and psychical need that he en-counters, for this is most natural to him. Once he asserts that "an imperious habit" forces him to do this. The poem "*Aber abseits wer ist's,*" [2] which is among the most touching of all that he has written, arose out of this concern for the lonely and the embittered.

Vogel, the physician, who is with him in the last years of his life, informs us that Goethe used to place at his disposal the means of helping the needy whom he encountered in his practice with something more than the ordinary aid. But he was not permitted to say from whom this generosity came.

So Goethe realizes a human ideal that he has summarized with the words "noble, helpful and good," an ideal whose charm and greatness lie in its splendid integrity and natu-ralness. As such it affected strongly those who saw it shin-ing out of his wonderful eyes; as such it affects us as we see it coming out of his life and his work.

The impression of Goethe's personality must have been great, indeed, for Wieland to describe him as "the greatest, best, most magnificent human being that God has ever cre-ated," and for Schiller to say of him that of all the people he had personally known Goethe was the man of greatest worth!

*

As the character of Goethe's human personality is molded by the profoundly natural, so also is the character of his cre-

---

[2] "But who is this man aloof."

ative being. With Goethe a bit of nature enters into literature. German poetry and poetry in general become in his
poetry for the first time natural, freed from everything that
is unnatural and finding their fulfilment in nature.

It is not by chance that a painter dwells in Goethe with
the poet. And if this painter, remarkable as he is, is not allowed to reach the heights, which he tries to conquer in ever
renewed attacks, none the less he collaborates with the poet
in his poetry. Goethe knows how to transplant us with
magic power into the nature which is there before his eyes
and his soul. He has the matchless talent of giving the seen
back to us as the experienced.

How wonderful indeed are his similes! He does not in-
vent an image to express a thought; instead of that pictures
of what he has seen and experienced wait within him for the
thought which is ordained to take form in them.

Nature is peculiarly dominant in Goethe's writing. In the
well-known epigram about the fact that mastery in paint-
ing was denied to him he comforts himself that he has
brought his special talent for writing German close to the
point of mastery. The mastery consists in this, that the German language comes to its most natural and perfect expression in him. It moves through his poetry with a strength
which is primitive and yet, at the same time, refined. It pre-
serves its perfect naturalness not only in form but also in
rhythm. It is never dominated by the rhythm of the meters
in which it appears, but expresses itself in complete freedom
within them and above them.

In accordance with the profound naturalness of his own
being Goethe finds his life bound to nature in an unbroken
spiritual union. The boy feels the need of worshipping God
at sunrise before an altar on which he has laid an offering of
fruit. When the first sorrow hits the fourteen-year-old boy
in the unjust suspicion which causes the loss of Gretchen,
he seeks comfort in the solitude of nature. He whispers to

her when his remorse over the injustice which he has done to Friederike will not give him rest. She is his confidante. In her he finds himself again.

If the friendship, by which men ordinarily encourage one another to do the good, and support one another in misfortune, lies so far in the background of Goethe's poetry, it is because his intimacy with nature is to him the great friendship beside which all other friendship pales.

To separate himself from nature is for him the greatest mistake into which man can fall. The tragic thought, therefore, which he enshrines in the Faust legend, and symbolizes through it, is that of alienation from nature. In magic arts, to which Faust applies himself, because by the methods previously tried he has not come close enough to nature to satisfy his overweening pretensions, he has abandoned nature and thereby has condemned himself to an existence that must wind up in error and guilt. Awaking after every erring experience to a new life in nature—these places are among the most gripping in the poetry of *Faust!*—still he resorts ever again to the magic spell, until at last there breaks through in his heart the longing to win again at any price a natural relationship with nature.

So the key to Goethe's drama of *Faust* lies in the lines:

"Noch hab' ich mich ins Freie nicht gekämpft.
Könnt' ich Magie von meinem Pfad entfernen,
Die Zaubersprüche ganz und gar verlernen,
Stünd' ich, Natur, vor dir, ein Mann allein,
Da wär's der Mühe wert, ein Mensch zu sein.
Das war ich sonst, eh' ich's im Düstern suchte. . . ." [3]

---

[3] "I have not yet fought through to liberty.
If I could from my path all witchcraft banish,
Let all the formulas of magic vanish,
Stood I a man before thee once again,
That would be worth, O Nature, all the pain.
A man I was before I sought the shadows."

Up to his last days Goethe lived in a constantly deepening communion with nature. He spends the day before his last birthday, when he has just finished *Faust* and has locked it up with a sevenfold seal, with his grandsons in the splendid late summer weather at Ilmenau, the place where nature has so often spread her peace over him. For the last time he reads on the wall of the hunting lodge his "Uber Allen Gipfeln ist Ruh," which he had written there in pencil on September 7, 1780. With mind refreshed, so Chancellor von Müller tells it, as though the peace of the woods and the cool breeze from the mountains had wafted a new breath of life into him, he returns, bearing within him a new appetite for work, which continues until his death.

*

United to nature in the most intimate fashion, Goethe is creative after the fashion of nature. Therein lies the peculiar greatness of his work, therein lie also its limitations. This is immediately manifest in his creative method. He does not set down in verse the splendor he experiences, but that splendor writes poetry in him. He can only work when the material calls him; when it no longer calls him, he is compelled to let it rest and wait until the call comes again. This way of the cross is the way he goes in his work and at the same time, full of wonder but quite free from envy, he watches Schiller, who is dependent only on his own will, and who could carry on his creative work constantly.

That the kind of natural and creative work for which he is suited sets boundaries and limitations for him he learns also from the fact that he is unable to express himself with equal freedom in every form of poetry. The power, the magic, and the inimitable perfection of his lyric, epic, and narrative poems spring from the fact that he is so deeply immersed in nature. That he cannot detach himself from her, stands in his way as a dramatic poet. He cannot bring himself to arrange nature and dramatic action for the best stage effects, but insists in letting them appear before the audience as they are found in reality. All of Goethe's pieces, therefore, so far as they are not in themselves suitable for the stage by virtue of the simplicity of the plot and the simplicity of the nature that appears in them, like *Tasso* and *Iphigenie*, have something that either fails to meet or surpasses the requirements of the stage. On the one hand they scorn current theatrical effects; on the other hand they make demands on the stage which far exceed its possibilities. Only on the stage of our imagination, for which they are really written, not upon the boards of the theater, can they reach their full effectiveness. However, this does not mean at all that they do not have their just claim to a place on the boards of the theater.

In his drastic manner Goethe breaks out on one occasion about the stage conventions, to which he cannot become reconciled, in words that are not justified, namely that one must abandon nature if he turns to the theater, and must be satisfied with "what can be performed for children by puppets in the midst of the laths, pasteboard and canvas of the platform."

One does not seek to correct with clever tricks of stagecraft that which is not suitable for the stage in Goethe and that which surpasses its possibilities, for this only makes more conspicuous the unbridged chasm between stage and reality which is found in him. Only the imagination of the spectator can lift what Goethe wishes to give him out of the imperfection and incompletion in which it greets him on the stage to a perfectly comprehended reality.

To what degree Goethe's ties with nature determine the magnitude and limits of his creative work is fully revealed in his material. Hardly ever has any prophecy concerning a poet been so completely fulfilled as the prophecy of

Merck, his pitilessly critical friend, who said to the young Goethe, that it was his unavoidable destiny to give poetic form to reality.

Indeed it is not granted to Goethe to infuse a material which is outside the range of his nature and his experience with feeling and poetry and so to let it take form in convincing vitality. He achieves perfection—and what a gripping and extraordinary perfection!—only when his work somehow is a revelation of himself. In *Dichtung und Wahrheit* he himself states that all of his works are fragments of a great confession. This is not only true of those books, like *Werther, Tasso, Faust, Wilhelm Meister,* in which a central figure appears embodying a bit of his own living soul. The other books also are in themselves a kind of creedal confession, since the very essence of them flows in the last analysis out of his experience. The more one penetrates into the details of Goethe's writings, the more one becomes aware how much of them is in the deepest sense a self-portrayal.

Whenever Goethe, without feeling himself under the moving compulsion of self-revelation, undertakes to treat any kind of theme poetically, something emerges which in spite of this or that excellence bears only vaguely the stamp of his spirit and his talent.

After he has taken over the management of the court theater at Weimar, he feels it to be his duty, as we learn from one of his letters, to write each year a few pieces suitable for the stage. So dubious plays appear like *Der Grosskophta, Der Bürgergeneral, Die Natürliche Tochter.* Later Goethe acknowledges that he is unable to carry through this undertaking, and conducts the theater for another half-generation without letting himself be tempted to any further dramatic writing.

The poet Goethe is not, then, a man who can do anything. If youth feels more drawn to Schiller than to him, as it always has felt drawn, this is to be explained not simply by the fact that it misses enthusiasm in him, but also by the fact that his works do not show the same perfection as Schiller's. It is hard for youth to tolerate the partly success- ful and the mediocre beside the most sublime.

In reality every creative spirit must submit to certain laws in defiance of which it cannot progress. Goethe in his mas- ter-works has perfectly fulfilled his mission of sharing with us this rich and noble nature of his, and therewith has made such a precious gift to us that it is unimportant to us to ask how far this gift might have been still further in- creased by other writings of a different kind.

*

And the content of this self-revelation? Three mutually related and closely associated motifs run along through it: the growth of nobility, the refining influence of woman, and the consciousness of guilt.

The growth of nobility. Since Goethe recognizes that the way he must travel for himself is a way of self-improve- ment, never forcing anything upon himself that is foreign to his nature, there do not appear in his books perfect heroes with an ardent idealism. Rather it is he himself who appears ever and again in different forms, striving with an incor- ruptible sense of reality to find through all his mistakes and failures the upward way.

All the characters which he draws—we think of those which pass before us in *Wilhelm Meister*—are basically imagined in process of purification, although each of them retains his own nature in it. This conception of growth in nobility shines forth with soft light in Goethe's simplest sentences, which throughout all time will illumine the way of questing mankind. He, who cherishes as the supreme wish of his life that the ideal of purity may become ever brighter within him, belongs to the pathfinders of humanity.

He consecrates woman as the one who helps to achieve nobility and to guard nobility, because she fulfils this mission in his own life.

Even his first love, Gretchen of Frankfort, takes advantage of the power which she exercises over him, to protect him from those stupidities which would have been beneath his dignity, and to keep him always loyally upright. Later Frau von Stein over a period of ten years is his guide on the way to purity and goodness. After that he receives help in his spiritual development from two princesses at the Weimar court and from other women who are not so conspicuous in the foreground of his life. Out of his life into his poetry these women go, therefore, now in scarcely altered attitude and form, now intermingling in new personalities.

So exalted characters appear like that of the Princess in *Tasso* and that of Iphigenie. To what heights in Goethe the old Iphigenia material rises through the way in which Iphigenia holds her brother and Pylades back from the path of violence, falsehood and hypocrisy, which they considered permissible for the attainment of freedom, and through the way in which she herself refuses to pay the price of ingratitude to attain it! We remember that in the original Greek version Iphigenia herself points out to the men the way of treachery!

There is hardly anything else in world literature which reaches the level of ethical power achieved in this work of Goethe's, and hardly anything else in which the ethical appears so simply and yet so forcefully.

As profoundly as he experiences the refining influence of women Goethe also experiences the consciousness of guilt. How the words in *Dichtung und Wahrheit* tremble, when later he speaks of the guilt-consciousness into which he has fallen through his behavior to Friederike! When, then, in *Götz*, in *Clavigo*, in *Stella*, and elsewhere, he produces a man who is guilty of imprudence towards a woman and subsequent inconstancy, it is not simply a poetic theme which he has found in his life and out of which he now makes literary capital, but a self-accusation, which will not let him rest.

The tragic guilt of the classics which a man incurs, not through any fault of his own but through inexorable necessity, does not appear in the poetry of Goethe. He sets before us only that which he has experienced, not that which he has imagined. Stark necessity cannot exist for the man who writes: "Our life, like the great whole in which we are contained, is made up in some incomprehensible manner of both freedom and necessity." It is particularly true, as he writes to Zelter in 1830, that he cannot get interested in a case of pure tragedy.

Goethe is well aware that in all the thoughts of guilt and guilt-consciousness with which we are occupied we are touching upon a great secret which we cannot comprehend and cannot fathom. He surmises, however, that the power which guilt seems to have over us is not appointed to destroy us, but in the end must contribute to our purification. Even over guilty men life insists upon its rights. "But man will live" are the words written at the end of the painful lines in *Dichtung und Wahrheit* which tell of his consciousness of guilt about Friederike, and then follows: "Therefore I openly took part in other. . . ." To be guilty means to possess a deeper and dearly bought understanding of things.

That earnestness arises from guilt Goethe proves in his own life. When the mature man cannot bear to banish again from his life a woman who has been brought into it through his guilt, but rather gives her a place beside him, accepting all the outer and inner difficulties which ensue for him, it is because the memory of that youthful guilty conscience is still vivid in him, and now points out to him the hard way which he has to go under the much more difficult circumstances of his present guilt. This is one aspect of the Christian chapter in Goethe's life which is too often over-

looked. One man, as we learn from one of his letters, understood Goethe's behavior. That man was Schiller.

How strongly, though all unobtrusively, the thought of
purification through guilt and the thought of sin and repara-
tion in men, which appear in Wilhelm Meister's years of
apprenticeship and travel, prove their validity!

When guilt begins to operate in a man he is on the way to
salvation through the unfathomable secret of love, which
penetrates into the darkness of earth like a beam of eternal
light.

> "Wer immer strebend sich bemüht,
> Den können wir erlösen." [4]

*

Goethe becomes manifestly a thinker in what he reveals
about himself as a poet. It is true that all his life long he
keeps away from the ranks of the philosophers. In one of his
epigrams he proudly boasts that he has been able to get on
so well only "because he has never reflected upon thinking."
He tries, indeed, to understand Kant, Hegel (towards whom
he has a genuine leaning) and Schelling, and endeavors,
wherever it is possible, to feel at one with them. But he does
not succeed. In the end he is always compelled to reaffirm
that they are traveling a road which is not his. He does not
comprehend the manner in which the German spirit wages
in these thinkers its strife for the ethical, idealistic world-
view.

Again it is his profound communion with nature in which
both the greatness and the limits of his poetry and thought
are fixed. In the last analysis he cannot go along with these
thinkers, no matter how much he tries, because their thinking stands between man and nature. Kant's *Critique of Pure
Reason* is, therefore, as he says, a prison, which prevents us
from enjoying nature in free poetry and thought. Systems of

---

[4] "He who strives onward constantly
Is not beyond our saving."

speculative philosophy are also a violation of nature to him.

His inner relationship with nature and his sense of reality do not permit him to treat her in this way. He approaches her with reverence, hoping that she may reveal to him some of her secrets, and may permit him to find that understanding in which strength for life lies. He is striving for a realistic, ethical nature philosophy.

When he writes in *Dichtung und Wahrheit:* "A light dawned upon men of lofty thought and spiritual feeling that the direct and first-hand view of nature, and behavior based upon such a view, are the best things that man could desire for himself, and are not at all difficult of attainment," he means thereby that striving for a world- and life-view to which he himself is devoted.

He will not let his thinking move around in an imaginary and endless circle. The teaching of metaphysics, as it usually goes, is but a vain word-wisdom for him. Only the eternal that appears to him when he submerges himself in nature and in himself has reality and meaning.

> "Willst du ins Unendliche schreiten,
>   Geh' nur im Endlichen nach allen Seiten." [5]

he declares in one of his utterances.

And how splendid is this other one:

> "Was ist Unendlichkeit?
>   Wie kannst du dich so quälen?
>   Geh in dich selbst!
>   Entbehrst du drin Unendlichkeit in Sein und Sinn
>   So ist dir nicht zu helfen." [6]

---

[5] "Wouldst thou even the endless know now,
Everywhere into the temporal go now."
[6] "What is eternity?
Why art thou so tormented?
Enter thyself!
And if in consciousness thou find'st the endless not,
Then is there naught to aid thee."

So he seeks for God not outside nature and coexistent with her, but within her alone. With Spinoza, whom he reveres as his philosophical teacher, he believes in the identity of God and nature. He lives by the conviction that God is in all things, and that all things are in God. He is reassured in this conviction by the saying of Greek wisdom about living and moving and being in God, a saying to which the apostle Paul refers, according to the Book of Acts, in his speech on the Areopagus at Athens. From his faith in God ring out these lines:

> "Ihm ziemt's, die Welt im Innern zu bewegen,
> Natur in sich, sich in Natur zu hegen,
> So dass, was in ihm lebt und webt und ist,
> Nie seine Kraft, nie seinen Geist vermisst." [7]

Goethe sees the appearance of piety in the fact that man gives spiritual expression in deed to this natural existence in God which he has in common with all being. This he expresses in the moving verses:

> "In unsers Busens Reine wogt ein Streben,
> Sich einem Hohen, Reinen, Unbekannten
> Aus Dankbarkeit freiwillig hinzugehen,
> Enträtselnd sich dem ewig Ungenannten,
> Wir heissen's: fromm sein." [8]

Because he knows this one thing, that he belongs to nature and to God, Goethe needs no artistically constructed world-view complete to the last detail, but is satisfied to

---

[7] "He rightly is the world's deep-centered motion,
   Nature and He in mutual devotion,
   So that what lives and moves and is in Him,
   Will never find His strength or spirit dim."
[8] "Within the pure of heart a yearning surges,
   A willing and a grateful resignation,
   Unto the high, the pure unknown it urges,
   Solving the nameless riddle of creation,
   We call it piety."

live with a world-view which is not complete and cannot be completed. He does not want to be richer than he can be through the absolutely honest acquisition of truth. With that he is confident that he can live.

He characterizes this attitude of his in the words: "To enter into every manifestation of the eternal, so far as it may be explored, to comprehend what may be explored down to its original elements, to reverence unassumingly what may not be explored." He dares to abide by the conviction that "nature is life and progression from some unknown center to some unrecognizable goal," and to rest confidently in the assurance "that nothing happens in the life of nature that is not in close harmony with the whole."

In this renunciation of any hope of a perfect world-view Goethe stands alone in his time. His old age falls in the decades when speculative philosophy, because it is confident that it can answer the ultimate questions, dominates the hearts of people and is regarded as the highest and final form of thinking.

How does Goethe, however, introduce ethics into his nature philosophy? The great problem for all nature philosophy—for him as for the Stoics, for Spinoza, for Lao-Tse, the Chinese thinker, with whom Goethe has so very much in common—is indeed how it proceeds from nature to ethics.

Here Goethe takes a very simple path. He does not bother about the derivation and origin of ethics, which the men of his time are attempting to explain, but takes the ethical thoughts which have appeared in mankind as a natural revelation. For, he says, Nature-God reveals itself not only in fundamental physical phenomena, but also in the fundamental phenomena of ethics. The ideas which appear in men are also manifestations of nature, in so far as the history of mankind is a part of the evolution of nature. Therefore, he is firmly convinced that in a way which we cannot explain to ourselves, the first cause of the world is at the same time the first cause of love, and that this love coming out of the eternal has a concern for us and wishes to find expression in us. So the wind of love blows through the thoughts of Goethe, as it comes out of the prophetical religion of Israel, and out of the religion of Jesus. He who saw even before Nietzsche that the great problem is how man's realization of nobility, which is self-realization, and his achievement of goodness are related to each other— and therein lies his own peculiar philosophical significance! —adopted the simple solution, that true self-realization can consist in nothing other than true realization of goodness. This conception of Goethe's concerning a nobility which is at the same time a generally accepted goodness, will become influential in the thought of mankind when Nietzsche's rebellion against the traditional notion of goodness which originated in mankind becomes little more than a reminder of the nineteenth century.

And what is the ideal of the perfect human being for the ethical thinker Goethe? A thoroughly simple one. We observe how small the life of Faust and the life of Wilhelm Meister turn out to be. Faust who demanded of the world-spirit complete knowledge of the world, spends his last days redeeming land from the sea which will produce fruit for men. Wilhelm Meister considers it his vocation to place himself at the service of refugees as a surgeon.

What is Goethe's man, of whom so many things have been said so obscurely? He is that for which Goethe strives in his own life: a man of deep sincerity, who at the same time is a man of deed, and as such is a strong but unobtrusive personality.

> "Dir selbst sei treu und treu den andern. . . ."
> "Und dein Streben sei's in Liebe,
>   Und dein Leben sei die Tat." [9]

---

[9] "To self be true, and true to others. . . ."
"Let thy search be in affection,
And thy living be thy deed."

Only that man can understand Goethe who falls under the spell of this deep and simple human ideal of his and is stirred by the spirit of resignation out of which it was born and which makes man fit for life.

*

This poet and thinker is for us a personality of universal validity, because at the same time he is, very significantly, still practically effective and active in the investigation of nature.

Our attention was at first so exclusively directed to the poet, that we did not give proper consideration to the meaning of the practical man and the nature student. Only through what the research of the last decades has brought to light concerning Goethe's life and creativity have we become accustomed to see him as he appeared to those who surrounded him in Weimar.

Goethe's governmental activities in the principality of Weimar are not of the kind that people like to suppose, namely that the poet's court office is just incidental in his life and that he does in it as much or as little as he feels like. He gives himself heart and soul to his job. With what great zeal from the very beginning did he devote himself to bringing order into the finances of the country! Even after his return from Italy, when a part of his work is taken away from him, and he continues to manage only those branches of the administration which have to do with art, science and public instruction, his office still makes great demands upon him. What an impression it makes upon a visitor, who in one of his last years finds him studying the figures of school attendance in all the districts of the arch-duchy of Sachen-Weimar! Seizing a pen Goethe at once calculates that school attendance has risen in general and is better in the mountainous regions than it is in the plain!

Natural science also is not just a hobby and a pastime to him, but a vocation. He has spent more time in his scientific work than in his poetry.

So the astonishing fact is that the active and scientific interests are as strong in him as the poetic ones.

Because in this sense he is really universal, we usually honor Goethe as the great posthumous son of the Renaissance. This is not true in every respect. He does, indeed, stand very close to some of the great characters of the Renaissance in his manifold talents, in his kinship with nature, in his yearning for truth, in the independence of his scientific research. At the same time, however, in the absence of enthusiasm, of restlessness, of revolutionary ideas, as everywhere in his whole spiritual being and in the earnestness of his interpretation of life, he is wholly different from them, and much less a man of the Renaissance than Leibnitz perhaps is.

The way, also, in which his manifold talents find expression is very different from the way of the Renaissance men. In the latter these talents burst into flame of themselves, as by spontaneous combustion, and disport and consume themselves in manifold and energetic activity. In Goethe these talents are brought into action, as we learn from himself, by the reflections which arise in him, and by the demands which life makes upon him.

He himself and others as well are aware that he has an eminently practical endowment. Lavater writes in 1774, a whole year before Goethe answers the call to Weimar: "Goethe would be a wonderful actor at the court of a prince; it is there that he belongs. He might have been a king."

And now, at the summit of his first poetic activity, already in the limelight of fame, he faces the question of what he should do with himself in the long pauses that occur, as he already knows from experience, between the periods of artistic creation. So he decides, as he himself says, "to devote himself to world affairs in order that none of his powers should be left unemployed."

The many-sided administrative duties, which for over a decade, from 1775 on, he carries on, involve a responsibility for highway construction, mining, regulation of rivers, and the encouragement of agriculture and forestry. In this work he was led to occupy himself more and more with nature after his scientific interests had found nourishment through his intercourse with doctors from the days of Leipzig and Strassburg on. In the end, then, nature, with which he comes into such close contact, takes complete possession of him. Everything that bears upon it—botany, mineralogy, geology, comparative anatomy, physics, chemistry—interests him.

In his own way—it could not be otherwise with his talents—he arrives at results which contemporary science reaches in another way. He is in advance of this science in many a perception, particularly in the insight, which natural science later verifies, that all forms of life in nature are mutually interdependent, and in conformity with the law of creation arise one out of the other.

In his attack, also, upon the view generally accepted at that time that mountains were all of volcanic origin he is right. We who are not involved in the controversial questions of that day are able to evaluate more justly than his contemporaries the contributions which Goethe made in his scientific writings, and we may say that they were worthy of him.

Goethe is a distinguished observer.

But is it not true that the officeholder and the nature-student have unduly suppressed the poet that lives in Goethe, and that so much which only the poet Goethe could create has never therefore been created? It is doubtless true that if the poet does not rouse himself to finish

Faust and *Wilhelm Meister* until the closing years of his life when his hand is already unsteady, the explanation is this, that the officeholder and the nature-student have not permitted him to undertake it earlier. Is not the fact, however, that we do not have these two books as the result of a single outpouring, outweighed by this other fact that they are now two streams in which the experience and thought of Goethe all the way from his youth to his old age are reflected?

Let us not forget that the poet has received at least one great gift from natural science. He is indebted to it for his friendship with Schiller. Had he not met Schiller, whom he wished to keep away from because he seemed too much of a revolutionary to him, at that memorable session of the Jena Society for Natural Science, they would never have gotten together at all. And how many of Goethe's most beautiful poems would have remained unborn in his soul without this friendship through which he became a poet once again, as he himself testifies!

Let us then leave it undecided whether that which the officeholder accomplished and the extent, great or little, to which Goethe contributed to the advancement of natural science, outweighs what he perhaps as a poet neglected on account of it. It all amounts to just this, that here also he was himself and in deep sincerity pursued a course which he had to take if he were true to his nature; that the great poet in his service as an officeholder and in his devoted work for natural science stands before us as a man who calls nothing great or small, but does everything that he undertakes with conscientiousness and devotion, is a living poem, in itself so moving that it could have been surpassed by no other that he might have given us in place of it. The most precious thing about a man, however great his creative activity may be, is always the man himself.

So the peculiar greatness of Goethe's universality con-

sists in the fact that it is the greatness of a well-rounded
and sincere man.

*

And now finally: What is Goethe's word to us, to us
human beings plunged as we are in terrible need? Has he
a special message for us?

Yes, he has.

All that thought in which a man embraces, not simply
the people of a single age, but humanity itself composed
of individual human beings—and this is true of Goethe's
thought as it is true of hardly any other—has something su-
perior to every age in it. Society is something temporal and
ephemeral; man, however, is always man.

So Goethe's message to the men of today is the same as
to the men of his time and to the men of all times: "Strive
for true humanity! Become yourself a man who is true to
his inner nature, a man whose deed is in tune with his
character."

But, the question rises, can we still achieve such human
personality in the midst of the frightful circumstances of
our day? Is the least sign of material and spiritual independence, which the individual must possess if he is to realize
this end, to be found among us? The circumstances of our
time are indeed such that material independence is hardly
known any more by the men of our day, and even their
spiritual independence is sorely threatened. All kinds of unnatural conditions are developing daily among us, in such a
way that man ceases to feel any longer that he is in every
respect a being that belongs to nature and to himself, and
becomes more and more a creature submissive to society.

So the question is raised which would have been considered impossible only a few decades ago: do we still desire to remain faithful to the ideal of human personality
even in the midst of hostile circumstances, or are we now

on the contrary loyal to a new ideal for humanity which ordains that man shall achieve a differently ordered fulfillment of his nature in the restless merging of his being in organized society?

What, however, can this mean except that we, like Faust, have erred terribly in detaching ourselves from nature and in surrendering ourselves to the unnatural?

After all what is now taking place in this terrible epoch of ours except a gigantic repetition of the drama of Faust upon the stage of the world? The cottage of Philemon and Baucis burns with a thousand tongues of flame! In deeds of violence and murders a thousandfold, a brutalized humanity plays its cruel game! Mephistopheles leers at us with a thousand grimaces! In a thousand different ways mankind has been persuaded to give up its natural relations with reality, and to seek its welfare in the magic formulas of some kind of economic and social witchcraft, by which the possibility of freeing itself from economic and social misery is only still further removed!

And the tragic meaning of these magic formulas, to whatever kind of economic and social witchcraft they may belong, is always just this, that the individual must give up his own material and spiritual personality and must live only as one of the spiritually restless and materialistic multitude which claims control over him.

That economic relations would some day eventuate in such a destruction of the independence of the individual, Goethe could not foresee. But with that capacity for mysterious foreboding in which he becomes aware of the danger of machinery, the early introduction of which he witnesses, he foresees that the spiritual independence of mankind will be threatened by the appearance of mob rule. This premonition is the basis for his unconquerable aversion to all revolutionaries. The revolutionary is for him the will of the masses bent on overthrowing the will of the individual.

Himself a witness of the earliest manifestations of mob rule in the French Revolution and in the wars for freedom, he is profoundly conscious that therewith something appears on the scene the consequences of which will be immeasureable. Therefore, the hesitant attitude toward the wars for freedom, which was the occasion of so many misunderstandings. He wants freedom for his people, of course, but the manifestation of the mass mind bent on it makes him feel very uneasy, as we learn from a conversation in 1813 with the history professor, Luden of Jena, in the course of which he reveals thoughts filled with profound emotion which at other times he keeps shut up within him.

Goethe is the first who feels something like a concern for man. At a time when others are still unconcerned, it dawns upon him that the great problem in the coming evolution of things will be this: how the individual can assert himself in the face of the multitude.

In this anxious foreboding, which he cherishes within him, and which lies behind many a stormy word which brought upon him the reproach that he was a reactionary and did not understand the signs of the time, there is also concern for his nation. He knows that no other nation so offends against its nature, in the renunciation by its own people of their spiritual independence, as his own nation, this people that he loves with such proud reserve. Yet he knows well, that the deep communion with nature, the spirituality, and the need for spiritual independence, which constitute his own being, are manifestations of the soul of his people in him.

And now, a hundred years after his death, it has come to pass, through a calamitous development determined by events and through the influence of that development upon the economic, the social, and the spiritual everywhere, that the material and the spiritual independence of the individual, so far as it is not already destroyed, is most seriously threat-

ened. We remember the death of Goethe in this most por-
tentous and fateful hour which has ever struck for mankind.
He is summoned as no other poet or thinker to speak to us
in this hour. He looks into our time as one most out of place
in it, for he has absolutely nothing in common with the
spirit in which it lives. But he comes with the most timely
counsel, for he has something to say to it which it is essential that it should hear.

What does he say to it?

He says to it, that the frightful drama that is being en-
acted in it can come to an end only when it sets aside the
economic and social magic in which it has trusted, when
it forgets the magic formulas with which it deludes itself,
when it is resolved to return at any cost to a natural relationship with reality.

To the individual he says: Do not abandon the ideal of
personality, even when it runs counter to developing circumstances. Do not give it up for lost even when it seems
no longer tenable in the presence of opportunistic theories
which would make the spiritual conform only to the material. Remain men in possession of your own souls! Do not
become human things which have offered hospitality to
souls which conform to the will of the masses and beat in
time with it.

Not everything in history is ordained to be overthrown
in the process of constant change, as it seems to superficial
observers; on the contrary, ideals that carry within themselves enduring worth will adjust themselves to changing
circumstances and grow stronger and deeper in the midst
of them. Such an ideal is that of human personality. If it is
given up, then the human spirit will be destroyed, which
will mean the end of civilization, and even of humanity.

Therefore, it is significant that in this time our eyes should
rest on Goethe, the messenger to true and noble humanity,
and that his thoughts should spread in every possible way

among the people. May his "be yourself" that resounds from them, and contains in this fateful hour for humanity the significance of an historical watchword for the world, make us brave to withstand the spirit of the time and even in the most difficult circumstances to preserve for ourselves and for others as much opportunity as possible for true humanity. And may it be true—for this is the critical thing!—that we, each of us in the measure of his given capacity, may also bring to pass the simple humanity of "let man be noble, kindly, and good," and that this ideal may be among us not simply as thought, but also as power.

*

Before two decades have come to an end, Frankfort will celebrate the two hundredth anniversary of the birthday of its greatest son. May it be that he who gives the memorial address at that new festival may be able to state that the deep darkness which surrounds this one has already begun to lighten, that a race with a true feeling for reality is seeking to comprehend it, and is beginning to achieve a mastery over material and social needs, united in its resolve to remain loyal to the one true ideal of human personality.

May the day dawn, then, in which the life of mankind once more flows along harmoniously, naturally, and with renewed vitality, like the music of Bach, with which Goethe was so greatly enchanted because his spirit reappeared in it.

Still, however, we stand under the doom of the words from *Hermann und Dorothea:*

> "Denn gelöst sind die Bande der Welt,
>   Wer knüpfet sie wieder
>   Als allein nur die Not, die höchste,
>   Die uns bevorsteht." [10]

---

[10] "For the bands of the world are all loosed,
    What ties them together
    But the need, need alone, the highest,
    That now confronts us."

So let the other fate rule over us also, and become truth for us, rising from the poem and finding expression in this new poetry:

"Aber es siege der Mut
In dem gesunden Geschlecht!" [11]

---

[11] "But now let fortitude rule
In the salubrious race!"

GOETHE

AN ADDRESS
DELIVERED AT THE GOETHE HOUSE
FRANKFORT ON THE MAIN
ON RECEIVING THE GOETHE PRIZE
FROM THE CITY OF FRANKFORT
AUGUST 28, 1928

I WILL NARRATE SHORTLY how I came into touch with Goethe, and how he reacted on my life.

It was in the field of philosophy that I had first to take up a position with regard to Goethe. When my revered Strassburg teachers, Wilhelm Windelband and Theodore Ziegler, had introduced me to the new philosophy, and I was glowing with enthusiasm for the great speculative systems, I could not but feel it almost incomprehensible that Goethe, who had lived through the powerful influence of a Kant, a Fichte, a Hegel, stood comparatively coldly on one side and let this influence pass by, while he remained within the circle of a nature-philosophy as he had learnt it from the Stoics and Spinoza, coming to believe in it with complete confidence and to attempt himself to develop it further. This astonishment at his remaining loyal to the apparently insignificant, and allowing something so powerful to pass by him, had a great effect on me. I can say that it was for me my first and longest-lasting incitement to come to an understanding with the new philosophy, and to develop my own thought. It thus became in the course of years clear to me that there are two philosophies which exist side by side. The object of all philosophy is to make us, as thinking beings, understand how we are to place ourselves in an intelligent and inward relation to the universe, and how we are to be active under the impulses which come to us from it.

The first of these philosophies brings man and the universe together only by doing violence to nature and the world, and putting men into connection with a world which has been made to bend itself to their thought.

The other philosophy, the insignificant nature-philosophy, leaves the world and nature as they are and compels man to find his place in them, and to assert himself in them as a spirit triumphant over them and working upon them.

The first is a work of genius, the other is elemental. The first progresses by means of mighty eruptions of thought such as appear in the great speculative systems of German philosophy and compel our admiration. But it has its day, and then disappears. The other, the homely, simple nature-philosophy, remains current. In it there comes into its own an elemental philosophizing which first sought to realize itself in the Stoic doctrine, but then shared the latter's ruin because it could not find its way through to an affirmative view of the world and of life. This nature-philosophy has been handed down to us incomplete. In Spinoza and in the rationalism of the eighteenth century it tried again to think itself through to world- and life-affirmation, but when it proved unable to do this, force took the place of tentative effort. The great speculative philosophy produced its systems of compulsion. But at a time when everyone was blinded by the sight of a world that was bent to human thought, there was one man who was not blinded but held to the elemental, homely nature-philosophy, recognizing that it had not yet indeed—that is, in the eighteenth century in which he lived—succeeded in thinking itself through to the end as affirmative, but knowing that it must somehow do so, and laboring on at that task in the plain and simple way which is the essence of his genius.

When I came to myself again and, returning to this nature-philosophy, recognized that what is demanded of us is to think it through to its goal of world- and life-affirmation in so simple a way that every thoughtful person in the world should have to take part in this thinking and thereby find himself at peace with the infinite, while at the same time obtaining an effective impulse to creative activity, then I saw in Goethe the man who had held out at the abandoned post where we were now mounting guard again, and resuming the interrupted work.

Meanwhile I found contact with him in another way. At the end of my student days I reread, almost by chance, the account of his *Harzreise* in the winter of 1777, and it made a wonderful impression on me that this man, whom we regarded as an Olympian, set out amid November rain and mist to visit a minister's son who was in great spiritual difficulties, and give him suitable help. A second time there was revealed to me behind the Olympian the deep but homely man. I was learning to love Goethe. And so whenever it happened in my own life that I had to take upon me some work or other in order to do for some fellow man the human service that he needed, I would say to myself, "This is a *Harzreise* for you."

I came once more on the real Goethe when it struck me in connection with his activities that he could not think of any intellectual employment without practical work side by side with it, and that the two were not held together by their character and object being similar, but were quite distinct and only united through his personality. It gripped me deeply that for this giant among the intellectuals there was no work which he held to be beneath his dignity, no practical employment of which he ever said that others on account of their natural gifts and of their profession could do it better than he, and that he was always ready to prove the unity of his personality by the union of practical work with intellectual activity.

I was already a minister when I first had to arrange my daily work, and when I sighed over the fact that through the much walking and the manifold duties entailed by my new office—which I had persisted in taking upon me to satisfy an inward need—I lost time which would have been available for intellectual labor, I comforted myself with Goethe, who, as we know, with mighty plans of intellectual activity in his head, would sit studying accounts and trying to set in order the finances of a small principality, examining plans so that streets and bridges should be constructed in the most practical way, and exerting himself year in, year out, to get disused mines at work again. And so this union of homely employment with intellectual activity comforted me concerning my own existence.

And when the life-course I had chosen led me to the point where I was compelled to embrace an activity which lay far from the natural endowment in which I had hitherto proved myself—far, too, from the employment for which I had prepared myself—then Goethe was the comforter who provided the words which helped me through. When other people, and even those who knew me best, found fault with my decision and tormented me with reproaches for wanting to study medicine, a subject for which (they said) I was not suited, declaring it to be a quixotic adventure, then I was able to reflect that this quixotic proceeding would perhaps not have been for him, the great man, so entirely quixotic, seeing that he finally allows his Wilhelm Meister, little prepared as he seemed to be for it, to become a surgeon in order that he may be able to serve. And at this point it struck me what a meaning it has for us all that Goethe in his search for the final destiny of man allows those characters in which he has depicted himself, viz. Faust and Wilhelm Meister, to end their days in a quite insignificant activity that they may thereby become men in the fullest sense in which, according to his ideas, they can become so.

Then when I began preparing myself for this new activity I met Goethe again. For my medical course I had to busy myself with natural science, though as a learner, not, like him, as an investigator. And how far removed, alas! lay natural science from what I hoped to complete in the way of intellectual production before I became immersed in practical work! But I was able to reflect that Goethe too had left intellectual work to return to the natural sciences. It had almost excited me that, at a time when he ought to have been bringing to its final shape so much that was stirring within him, he lost himself in the natural sciences. And now I myself, who had hitherto been engaged only in intellectual work, was compelled to occupy myself with them. It deepened my nature, and it became clear to me why Goethe devoted himself to them and would not give them up. It was because it means for everyone who produces intellectually, enlightenment and enormous gain, if he who has hitherto created facts now has to face facts, which are something, not because one has imagined them, but because they exist. Every kind of thinking is helped, if at any particular moment it can no longer occupy itself with what is imagined but has to find its way through reality. And when I found myself under this "On through reality!" compulsion, I could look back at the man who had done it all before us.

Again when my laborious years of study had ended, and I left them behind as a qualified doctor, I once more met Goethe, seeming even to converse with him in the primeval forest. I had always supposed that I went out there as a doctor, and in the first years, whenever there was building or similar work to be done, I took care to put it on the shoulders of those who seemed to me to be specially adapted for it, or who had been engaged for it. But I had to acknowledge that this would not do. Either they did not turn up or they were so ill-suited for the work that no progress was made. So I accommodated myself to the work, far removed though it was from my duties as a doctor. But the worst came last. When at the end of 1925, owing to a severe famine which endangered the existence of my hospital, I was compelled to get a plantation made for it, so that during any famine in the future we might be able to keep our heads above water to some extent through our own resources, I was obliged to superintend the clearing of the forest myself. The very miscellaneous body of workers which the chance of the moment produced from among the willing ones of the friends of our patients would bow to no authority but that of "the old Doctor," as I was called. So I stood for weeks and months in the forest, worrying over refractory laborers, in order to wrest from it land that would produce food for us. Whenever I got reduced to despair I thought how Goethe had devised for the final activities of his Faust the task of winning from the sea land on which men could live and feed themselves. And thus Goethe stood at my side in the swampy forest as my smiling comforter, and the man who really understood.

There is one more point which I should like to mention of Goethe's influence on me, and it is this: that I found him everywhere haunted by anxiety about justice. When about the end of the last century the theory began to prevail that whatever is to be realized must be realized without regard to right, without regard to the fate of those who are hard hit by the change, and I myself did not know how these theories should be met, it was to me a real experience to find everywhere in Goethe the longing to avoid realizing any design at the cost of right. And I have again and again with real emotion turned over the final pages of *Faust* (which both in Europe and in Africa I always reread at Easter) where Goethe represents as the last experience of Faust, and that in which he is for the last time guilty of wrongdoing, his attempt to remove the hut which disturbs him in his possession—by a slight and well-intentioned act of violence—being, as he himself says, tired of righteousness. But in the execution of it this well-intentioned act of violence becomes a cruel act of violence in which more than one person loses his life, and the hut goes up in flames. That Goethe at the conclusion of his *Faust* should insert this episode, which holds up the action of the poem, gives us a deep insight into the way in which there worked within him anxiety about justice, and the strong desire to realize any plan that has to be carried out without causing any kind of injury.

My final lasting contact with Goethe arose out of my recognition of the living and vigorous way in which he shared the life of his age in its thought and in its activity. Its billows were ever surging within him. That is what impresses one, not only in the young and in the fully ripe Goethe, but in the aged Goethe also. When the mail coach was still crawling along the high road, and we should have thought that the industrial age could be announcing its arrival merely by uncertain shadows cast in advance, it was for him already there. He was already concerning himself with the problem it put before the world, viz. that the machine was now taking the place of the man. If in his *Wilhelm Meister* he is no longer master of his material, it is not because the old man no longer has the power to shape it which he formerly had at his command, but because the material had grown till it could be neither measured nor moulded; it was because the old man was putting into it the whole of his experience and of his anxiety about the future; it was because this old man was so concerned about being among the men of his age as one who understands the new age and has grown to be a part of it. That is what impresses one so deeply in the aging Goethe.

Such were the contacts with Goethe through which I came nearer and nearer to him. He is not one who inspires. He puts forward in his works no theories which rouse to enthusiasm. Everything that he offers is what he himself has experienced in thought and in events, material which he has worked up into a higher reality. It is only through experience that we come nearer to him. Through experience which corresponds with his he becomes to us instead of a stranger a confidant with whom we feel ourselves united in reverential friendship. My own destiny has brought it about for me that I can experience with a vividness that goes to the very marrow of my soul the destinies of our time and anxiety about our manhood. That in an age when so many whom we need as free personalities get imprisoned in the work of a profession I can feel all these things as such a free personality, and, like Goethe, can through a happy combination of circumstances serve my age as a free man, is to me an act of grace which lightens my laborious life. Every task or piece of creative work that I am allowed to do is to me only a return of gratitude to destiny for that act of grace.

Similar anxiety about his age and similar work for it Goethe went through before us. Circumstances have become more chaotic than he, even with his clear vision, could foresee. Greater, then, than circumstances must our strength be, if in the midst of them we are to become men who understand our age and grow to be a part of it.

A spirit like Goethe's lays upon us three obligations. We have to wrestle with conditions so as to make it secure that men who are imprisoned in work and are being worn out by it may nevertheless preserve the possibility of a spiritual existence. We have to wrestle with men so that in spite of being continually drawn aside to the external things which are provided so abundantly for our age, they may find the road to inwardness and keep in it. We have to wrestle with ourselves and with all and everything around us, so that in a time of confused ideals which ignore all the claims of humanity we may remain faithful to the great humane ideals of the eighteenth century, translating them into the thought of our own age, and attempting to realize them to-day. That is what we have to do, each of us in his life, each of us in his profession, in the spirit of the great Frankfort child whose birthday we are celebrating to-day in his birthplace. I myself think that this Frankfort child does not move further away from us with the course of time, but comes nearer to us. The further we travel forward the more certainly we recognize Goethe to be the man who, as our own duty is, amid the deep and widely varied experience of his age cared for his age and labored for it; the man who would become a man who understood his age and grew to be a part of it. He did this with the abounding talents which were laid in his cradle here by destiny. We have to do it as men who have received only one small pound but who in our trading with that pound wish to be found faithful. So may it be!

INDEX

Date Due

DEMCO-293

FE 15 '53		
NO 10 59		
NO -2 69		
FE 9 '83		